D0122108

THE PATH TO
·INNER
PEACE

*Inspirational Thoughts
for Everyday Living*

Compiled by Maggie Pinkney

The Five Mile Press

The Five Mile Press
22 Summit Road
Noble Park Victoria 3174
Australia

Published in 2002

This compilation © The Five Mile Press

Design: Zoë Murphy
Calligraphy and borders: Lynne Muir

Printed by Toppan in Hongkong

National Library of Australia Cataloguing-in-Publication data

The path to inner peace: inspirational thoughts

ISBN 1 86503 325 1.

1. Religion - Quotations, maxims, etc. 2. Spirituality - Quotations, maxims, etc.
3. Self-actualisation (Psychology) I. Pinkney, Maggie.

291.43

CONTENTS

Introduction

Keep a green tree in your heart and perhaps a singing bird will come.

CHINESE PROVERB

INTRODUCTION

Most of us live in a world regulated by clocks and schedules. Our senses are daily besieged by noisy traffic, garish advertisements and endless streams of information. Given all this, it's not surprising that we lose our childhood connection to the simplicity of nature and the wellsprings of the universe – and that we gradually become alienated from our true selves.

The profound thoughts in this inspirational anthology have been chosen to help you focus inward – to reclaim the essence of your spiritual being. The recuperative power of moments of solitude – time out to get in touch with your inner self – has been extolled by writers and thinkers down the ages, from the Roman philosopher Marcus Aurelius to Swiss-born psychiatrist Elisabeth Kübler-Ross.

This book will help you to cultivate the habit of listening to your own innate wisdom – to what the English poet Robert Browning calls 'the inmost centre in us all, where truth abides in fullness'. Insights into ways of setting aside anger and bitterness, and overcoming self-doubt and depression are also included.

The reflections, benedictions and philosophical truths that make up this anthology have been gleaned from a wide variety of sources – ranging from sacred texts to the works of poets, writers and thinkers from many different cultures and religions. Dip into this distilled wisdom, and find the key to your own source of inner peace – surely life's most precious gift.

THE
SILENCE
WITHIN

Learn to get in touch with the silence within yourself and know that everything in this life has a purpose. There are no mistakes, no coincidences; all events are blessings given to us to learn from.

•

ELISABETH KÜBLER-ROSS, b. 1926
Swiss-born American psychiatrist and writer

In the rush and noise of life,
as you have intervals,
step home within yourself and be still.
Wait upon God,
and feel his good presence;
this will carry you evenly through
your day's business.

•

WILLIAM PENN, 1644–1718
English Quaker and founder of Pennsylvania, USA

Solitude —
walking alone, doing things alone —
is the most blessed thing in the world.
The mind relaxes
and thoughts begin to flow
and I think that I am beginning
to find myself a little.

•

HELEN HAYES, 1900–1993
American actress

Pearls lie not on the seashore.
If thou desirest one
thou must dive for it.

•

CHINESE PROVERB

There is nobody else like you.
The more you can quiet your own
thoughts, fears, doubts and suspicions,
the more will be revealed to you from
the higher realms of imagination,
intuition and inspiration.

•

KENNETH WYDRO, b. 1933
American lecturer

Living in solitude till the fullness of time,

I still kept the dew of my youth

and the freshness of my heart.

·

NATHANIEL HAWTHORNE, 1804–1864

American novelist and short story writer

The more faithfully you listen
to the voice within you,
the better you will hear
what is sounding outside.

•

DAG HAMMARSKJÖLD, 1905–1961
Swedish ambassador, UN Secretary-General

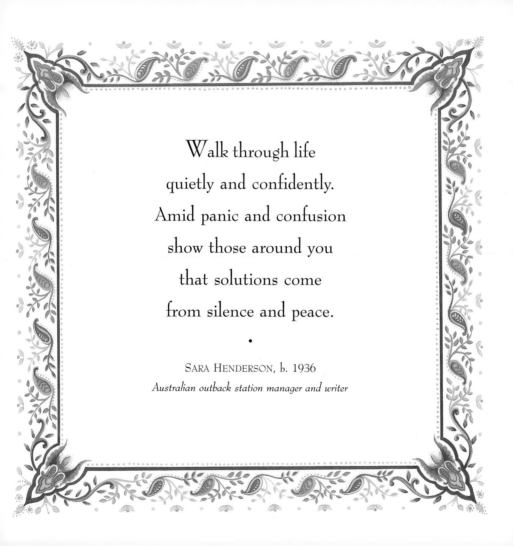

Walk through life
quietly and confidently.
Amid panic and confusion
show those around you
that solutions come
from silence and peace.

·

SARA HENDERSON, b. 1936
Australian outback station manager and writer

There is no need to go to India
or anywhere else to find peace.
You will find that deep place of silence
right in your room, your garden
or even your bathtub.

•

ELISABETH KÜBLER-ROSS, b. 1926
Swiss-born American psychiatrist and writer

Men seek out retreats for themselves, cottages in the country, lonely seashores and mountains. Thou too art disposed to hanker greatly after such things. And yet all this is foolishness, for it is within thy power whenever thou wilt, to retire into thyself; and nowhere is there any place whereto a man may retire quieter and more free from politics than his own soul.

•

MARCUS AURELIUS, 121–180 AD
Roman emperor and philosopher

When I begin to sit
with the dawn in solitude,
I begin to really live.
It makes me treasure
every single moment
of life.

•

GLORIA VANDERBILT, 1924–1997
American actress and fashion designer

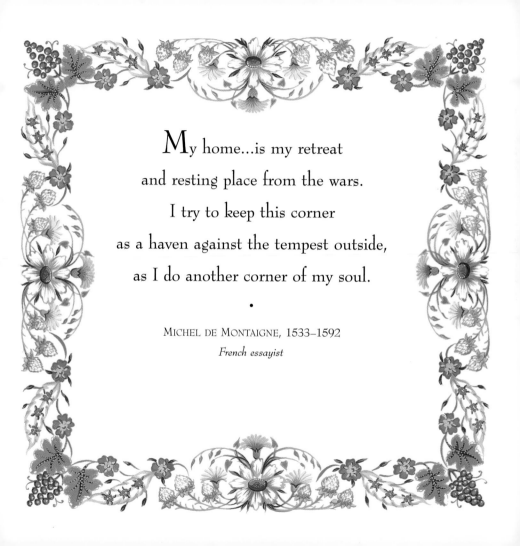

My home...is my retreat
and resting place from the wars.
I try to keep this corner
as a haven against the tempest outside,
as I do another corner of my soul.

•

MICHEL DE MONTAIGNE, 1533–1592
French essayist

Go cherish your soul;

expel companions;

set your habits to a life of solitude;

then will the faculties rise

fair and full within.

•

RALPH WALDO EMERSON, 1803–1882

American essayist, poet and philosopher

Genuine tranquillity of the heart and perfect peace of mind, the highest blessings on earth after health, are to be found only in solitude and, as a permanent disposition, only in the deepest seclusion.

•

ARTHUR SCHOPENHAUER, 1788–1860
German philosopher

*Arranging a bowl of flowers in the morning
can give a sense of quiet to a crowded day —
like writing a poem or saying a prayer.
What matters is that one be for a time
inwardly attentive.*

•

ANNE MORROW LINDBERGH, b. 1906
American writer

'A STILL
AND QUIET
CONSCIENCE'

A peace above all earthly dignities,

A still and quiet conscience.

•

WILLIAM SHAKESPEARE, 1564–1616
English playwright and poet

*S*ome good must come by clinging to the right. Conscience is a man's compass, and though the needle sometimes deviates, though one perceives irregularities in directing one's course by it, still one must try to follow its direction.

•

VINCENT VAN GOGH, 1853–1890
Dutch post-impressionist painter

He that loses his conscience

has nothing left

that is worth keeping.

•

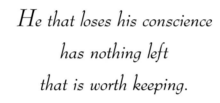

ISAAK WALTON, 1593–1683
English writer

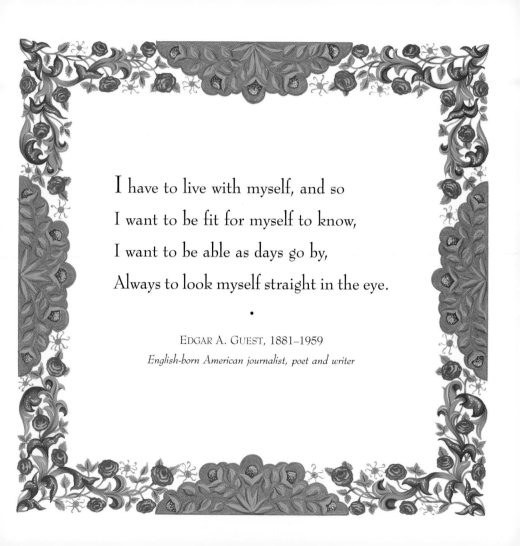

I have to live with myself, and so
I want to be fit for myself to know,
I want to be able as days go by,
Always to look myself straight in the eye.

•

EDGAR A. GUEST, 1881–1959
English-born American journalist, poet and writer

A man cannot be comfortable
without his own approval.

•

MARK TWAIN, 1835–1910

American writer and humorist

I desire to so conduct my affairs of this administration that if at the end, when I come to lay down the reins of power, I have lost every other friend on earth, I shall at least have one friend left, and that friend shall be down inside of me.

•

ABRAHAM LINCOLN, 1809–1865
President of the United States of America

The voice of conscience is so delicate that it is easy to stifle it, but it is also so clear that it is impossible to mistake it.

•

MME ANNE DE STAËL, 1766–1817
French writer and critic

DEPRESSION
& SELF-DOUBT

*Noble deeds and hot baths
are the best cures
for depression.*

•

DODIE SMITH, 1896–1990
English writer

How to be happy when you
are miserable. Plant Japanese poppies
with cornflowers and mignonette,
and bed out the petunias among the
sweet-peas so they shall scent each other.
See the sweet-peas coming up.

•

RUMER GODDEN, b. 1907
English writer

I will tell you what I have learned for myself.

For me a long, five or six mile walk helps.

And one must go alone and every day.

•

BRENDA UELAND, 1891–1986

American writer

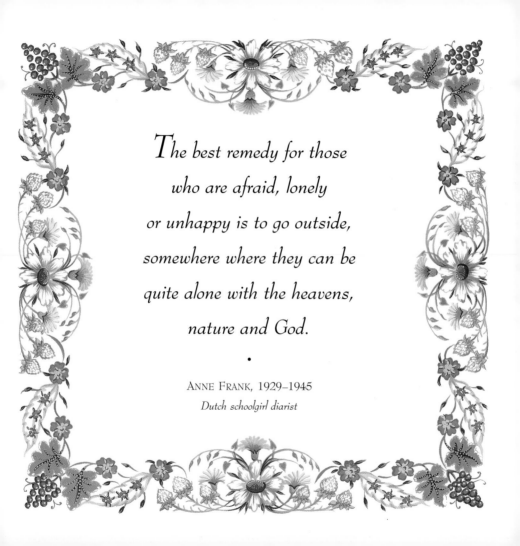

The best remedy for those who are afraid, lonely or unhappy is to go outside, somewhere where they can be quite alone with the heavens, nature and God.

•

ANNE FRANK, 1929–1945
Dutch schoolgirl diarist

We can be cured of depression in only fourteen days if every day we will try to think of how we can be helpful to others.

•

ALFRED ADLER, 1870–1937
Austrian psychiatrist

Be gentle with yourself.
If you will not be your own
unconditional friend, who will be?
If you are playing an opponent and
you are also opposing yourself —
you are going to be outnumbered.

•

DAN MILLMAN
American writer

And above all things, never think
that you're not good enough yourself.
A man should never think that.
My belief is that in life people will
take you at your own reckoning.

•

ANTHONY TROLLOPE, 1815–1882
British novelist

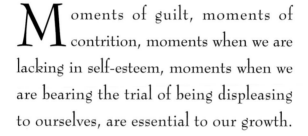

M oments of guilt, moments of
contrition, moments when we are
lacking in self-esteem, moments when we
are bearing the trial of being displeasing
to ourselves, are essential to our growth.

•

M. SCOTT PECK, b. 1936
American psychiatrist and writer

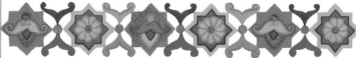

Y ou who perceive yourself as weak and frail,
with futile hopes and devastated dreams,
born but to die, to weep and suffer pain, hear this:
all power is given to you in earth and heaven.
There is nothing you cannot do.

•

A Course in Miracles

Whether living alone
is adventure or hardship
will depend entirely on
your attitude and your decisions.
Become friends with yourself;
learn to appreciate who you are
and your unique gifts.
Be patient with yourself
and use your sense of humour to keep
things in perspective.

•

DOROTHY EDGERTON, b. 1911
American writer

It is almost impossible to remember
how tragic a place the world
is when one is playing golf.

•

Robert Lynd, 1879–1949
Irish essayist and journalist

Prayers & Benedictions

God

grant me the serenity to
accept the things
that I cannot change,
the courage to change
the things that I can,
and the wisdom to distinguish
the one from the other.

•

REINHOLD NIEBUHR, 1892–1971

American theologian

Oh Lord, help me

To be calm when things go wrong,

To persevere when things are difficult,

To be helpful to those in need,

And to be sympathetic to those

whose hearts are heavy.

•

ANONYMOUS

Let there be many windows in your soul,

That all the glories of the universe

May beautify it.

•

RALPH WALDO TRINE, 1866–1958
American poet and writer

*T*each us delight in simple things,

And mirth that has no bitter springs;

Forgiveness free of evil done,

And love to all men 'neath the sun.

•

RUDYARD KIPLING, 1865–1936
Indian-born British writer and poet

*T*each me to feel another's woe,

To hide the fault I see;

That mercy I to others show,

That mercy show to me.

•

ALEXANDER POPE, 1688–1744
English poet

Let nothing disturb you.

Let nothing frighten you.

Everything passes away

except God.

•

St Theresa, 1515–1582
Spanish nun

Deep peace of the running wave to you.

Deep peace of the flowing air to you.

Deep peace of the quiet earth to you.

Deep peace of the shining stars to you.

Deep peace of the Son of Peace to you.

·

CELTIC BENEDICTION

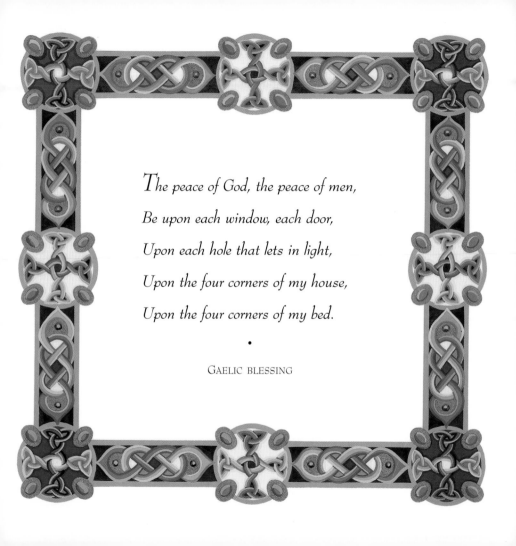

The peace of God, the peace of men,

Be upon each window, each door,

Upon each hole that lets in light,

Upon the four corners of my house,

Upon the four corners of my bed.

•

GAELIC BLESSING

Let me be a little kinder,
Let me be a little blinder
To the faults of those around me.

•

EDGAR A. GUEST, 1881–1959
English-born American journalist, poet and author

O Thou who art at home

Deep in my heart

Enable me to join you

Deep in my heart.

•

THE TALMUD

O God,

help us not to despise or oppose

what we do not understand.

•

WILLIAM PENN, 1644–1718
English Quaker and founder of Pennsylvania, USA

STRENGTH
IN
ADVERSITY

Have courage for the greatest sorrows of life and patience for the small ones, and when you have accomplished your daily task, go to sleep in peace. God is awake.

·

VICTOR HUGO, 1802–1885
French poet and writer

We deem those happy
who from the experience of life
have learned to bear its ills
without being overcome by them.

•

CARL JUNG, 1875–1961
Swiss psychiatrist

You have to accept
whatever comes along
and the only important thing is
that you meet it with
the best you have to give.

•

ELEANOR ROOSEVELT, 1884–1962
First Lady of the United States of America and UN delegate

Of all the liars in the world,
sometimes the worst
are your own fears.

•

RUDYARD KIPLING, 1865–1936
Indian-born British writer and poet

Fearlessness may be a gift, but perhaps more
precious is the courage acquired through endeavour,
courage that comes from cultivating the habit
of refusing to let fear dictate one's actions,
courage that could be described as 'grace under pressure'
— grace which is renewed repeatedly
in the face of harsh, unremitting pressure.

•

AUNG SAN SUU KYI, b. 1945
*Burma's democratically elected leader
and winner of the Nobel Peace Prize*

Expect trouble as an inevitable part of life, and when it comes, hold your head high, look it squarely in the eye and say, 'I will be be bigger than you. You cannot defeat me.' Then repeat to yourself the most comforting words of all, 'This too will pass.'

•

ANN LANDERS, b. 1918
American advice columnist

When you are up against a problem, try and eliminate all your personal feelings and emotions as the first step in the solving process and you will probably find you have eliminated the problem.

•

SARA HENDERSON, b. 1936
Australian outback station manager and writer

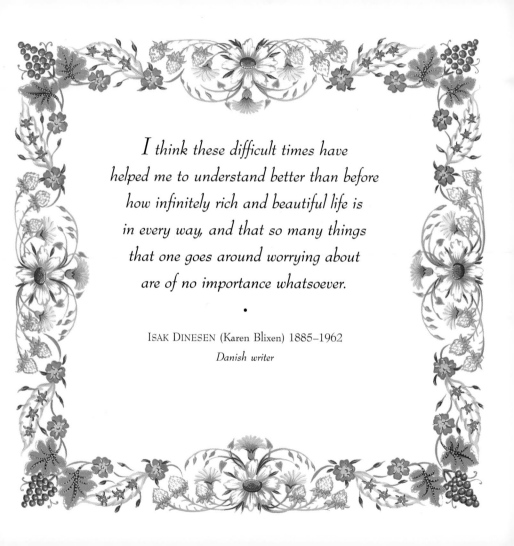

*I think these difficult times have
helped me to understand better than before
how infinitely rich and beautiful life is
in every way, and that so many things
that one goes around worrying about
are of no importance whatsoever.*

•

ISAK DINESEN (Karen Blixen) 1885–1962
Danish writer

Life affords no higher pleasure
than that of surmounting difficulties,
passing from one step of success
to another, forming new wishes
and seeing them gratified.

•

SAMUEL JOHNSON, 1709–1784

English lexicographer, critic and writer

Problems call forth our courage and our wisdom; indeed they create our courage and our wisdom. It is only because of problems that we grow mentally and spiritually. It is through the pain of confronting and resolving problems that we learn.

·

M. SCOTT PECK, b. 1936
American psychiatrist and writer

I believe anyone can conquer fear by doing the things he fears to do, provided he keeps doing them until he gets a record of successful experiences behind him.

•

ELEANOR ROOSEVELT, 1884–1962
First Lady of the United States of America and UN delegate

'TO THINE
OWN SELF
BE TRUE'

This above all — to thine own self be true,

And it must follow, as the night the day,

Thou canst not then be false to any man.

•

WILLIAM SHAKESPEARE, 1564–1616
English poet and playwright

*E*very human is intended

to have a character of his own;

to be what no others are,

and to do what no other can do.

•

WILLIAM ELLERY CHANNING, 1780–1842

American clergyman

Your vision will become clear only

when you can look into your heart.

Who looks outside, dreams.

Who looks inside, awakes.

•

CARL JUNG, 1875–1961
Swiss psychiatrist

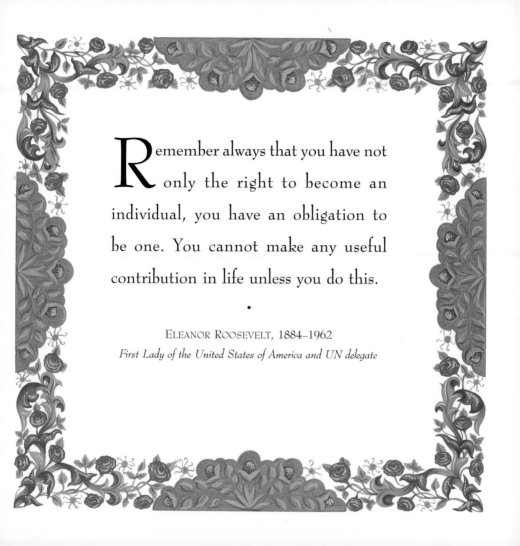

Remember always that you have not only the right to become an individual, you have an obligation to be one. You cannot make any useful contribution in life unless you do this.

•

ELEANOR ROOSEVELT, 1884–1962
First Lady of the United States of America and UN delegate

To be what we are, and to become what we are capable of becoming is the only end in life.

•

One just has to be oneself.
That's my basic message.
The moment you accept yourself as you are,
all burdens, all mountainous burdens,
simply disappear.
Then life is a sheer joy,
a festival of lights.

•

BHAGWAN SHREE RAJINEESH
Indian spiritual leader

Resolve to be thyself; and know that he

Who finds himself loses his misery.

•

MATTHEW ARNOLD, 1822–1888

English poet, critic and essayist

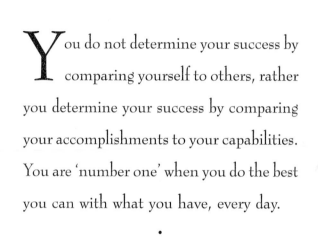

Y ou do not determine your success by comparing yourself to others, rather you determine your success by comparing your accomplishments to your capabilities. You are 'number one' when you do the best you can with what you have, every day.

·

ZIG SIGLAR

American motivational writer

Truth is within ourselves; it takes no rise

From outward things, what'er you may believe.

There is an inmost centre in us all,

Where truth abides in fullness.

•

ROBERT BROWNING, 1812–1889
English poet

One person's definition of success is another person's first step. Only you can rate your accomplishments, and find peace within yourself.

·

ANONYMOUS

Every man

has to seek in his own way to make

his own self more noble

and to realise his own true worth.

•

ALBERT SCHWEITZER, 1875–1965

French medical missionary

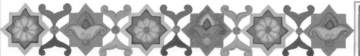

Know your own true worth,
and you shall not perish..
God has given you Knowledge,
so that by its light
you may not only worship Him,
but also see yourself
in your weakness and strength.

•

KAHLIL GIBRAN, 1882–1931
Lebanese poet, artist and mystic

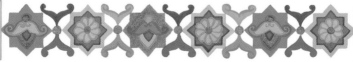

Never be afraid to tread the path alone. Know which is your path and follow it wherever it may lead you; do not feel you have to follow in someone else's footsteps.

•

EILEEN CADDY

Co-founder of the Findhorn Foundation, Scotland

If a man does not keep pace with his companions, perhaps it is because he hears a different drummer. Let him step to the music which he hears, however measured or far away.

•

HENRY DAVID THOREAU, 1817–1862
American essayist and writer

Once read thy own breast right,

And thou hast done with fears!

Man gets no other light,

Search he a thousand years.

•

MATTHEW ARNOLD, 1822–1888
English poet and critic

PEACE & CONTENTMENT

O gift of God! a perfect day,

Whereon shall no man work but play,

Whereon it is enough for me

Not to be doing but to be.

•

HENRY WADSWORTH LONGFELLOW, 1807–1882

American poet and writer

Let us not therefore go hurrying about and collecting honey, bee-like, buzzing here and there impatiently from a knowledge of what is to be arrived at. But let us open our leaves like a flower, and be passive and receptive.

•

JOHN KEATS, 1795–1821
English poet

The day, water, sun, moon, night —

I do not have to pay

to enjoy these things.

•

TITUS MACCIUS PLATUS, c. 254–184 BC

Roman dramatist

If I had two loaves of bread,
I would sell one and buy hyacinths,
For they would feed my soul.

•

THE KORAN

I like to walk about among the
beautiful things that adorn the world;
but private wealth I should decline,
or any sort of personal possessions,
because they would take away
my liberty.

•

GEORGE SANTAYANA, 1863–1952
Spanish-born American philosopher

Under this tree, where light and shade
   Speckle the grass like a Thrush's breast,
Here, in this green and quiet place,
   I give myself to peace and rest.
The peace of my contented mind,
   That is to me a wealth untold —
When the Moon has no more silver left,
   And the Sun's at the end of his gold.

•

W.H. DAVIES, 1871–1940
Welsh poet, writer and tramp

Sweet are the thoughts
that savor of content;
The quiet mind
is richer than a crown.

•

ROBERT GREENE, 1558–1592
English poet

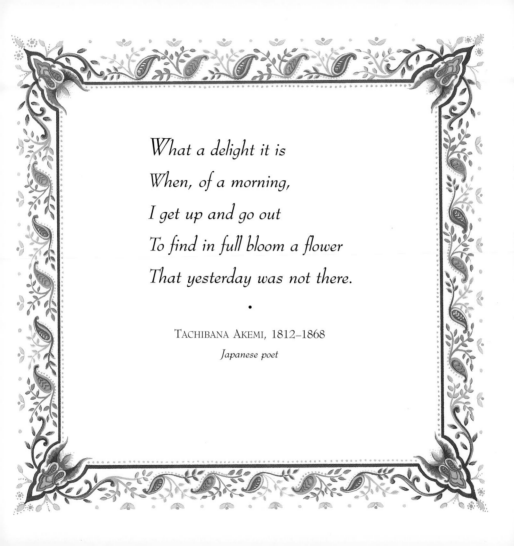

What a delight it is
When, of a morning,
I get up and go out
To find in full bloom a flower
That yesterday was not there.

•

TACHIBANA AKEMI, 1812–1868
Japanese poet

Yes, in the poor man's garden grow

Far more than herbs and flowers —

Kind thoughts, contentment, peace of mind,

And joy for weary hours.

•

MARY HOWITT, 1799–1888
English author

One is nearer God's Heart

in a garden,

Than anywhere else on earth.

•

DOROTHY FRANCES GURNEY, 1858–1932
English poet

He is happiest,

be he king or peasant,

who finds peace in his home.

•

Johann von Goethe, 1749–1832

German writer, dramatist and scientist

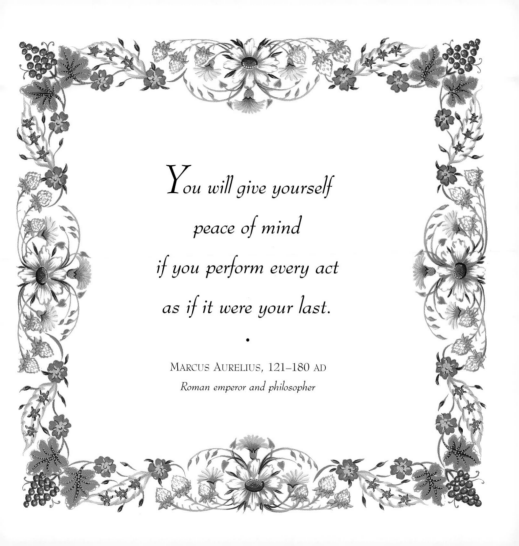

*Y*ou will give yourself

peace of mind

if you perform every act

as if it were your last.

·

MARCUS AURELIUS, 121–180 AD

Roman emperor and philosopher

Peace is not an absence of war,

it is a virtue, a state of mind,

a disposition for benevolence,

confidence, justice.

•

BENEDICT SPINOZA, 1632–1677
Dutch philosopher

Who loves a garden

still his Eden keeps,

Perennial pleasures, plants and

wholesome harvest reaps.

•

AMOS BRONSON ALCOTT, 1799–1888
American teacher and philosopher

Health is the greatest gift,

contentment the greatest wealth,

faithfulness the best relationship.

•

BUDDHA, c. 563–483 BC
Indian religious leader and founder of Buddhism

A person who is not disturbed
by the incessant flow of desires
can alone achieve peace,
and not the man who strives
to satisfy such desires.

•

BHAGAVAD GITA

To be content, look backward
on those who possess less than yourself,
not forward to those who possess more.

•

BENJAMIN FRANKLIN, 1706–1790
American statesman and scientist

Drink tea

and forget

the world's noises.

·

CHINESE SAYING

I am indeed rich,

since my income is superior

to my expense, and my expense

is equal to my wishes.

•

EDWARD GIBBON, 1737–1794
English historian and politician

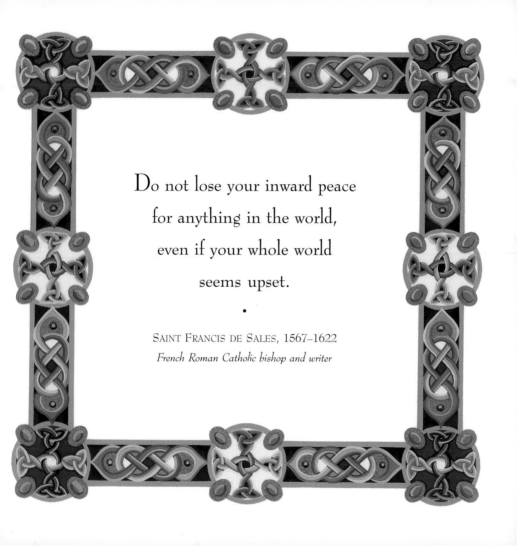

Do not lose your inward peace
for anything in the world,
even if your whole world
seems upset.

•

SAINT FRANCIS DE SALES, 1567–1622
French Roman Catholic bishop and writer

Quiet by day,
  Sound sleep by night: study and ease
Together mixed; sweet recreation,
  And innocence, which most does please
With meditation.
  Thus let me live, unseen, unknown;
Thus unlamented let me die;
  Steal from the world, and not a stone
Tell where I lie.

•

ALEXANDER POPE, 1688–1744
English poet

To live content with small means; to seek elegance rather than luxury; and refinement rather than fashion...to bear all cheerfully, do all bravely, await occasions, hurry never. In a word to let the spiritual, unbidden and unconscious grow up through the common. This is to be my symphony.

•

WILLIAM ELLERY CHANNING, 1780–1842
American minister

He is richest
who is content with the least,
for content is the wealth
of nature.

•

SOCRATES, 468–399 BC
Greek philosopher

A Matter of Faith

In the midst of outer dangers I have felt an inner calm and known resources of strength that only God could give... Behind the harsh appearances of the world there is a benign power.

•

MARTIN LUTHER KING, 1929–1968
American civil rights leader and Baptist minister

I believe that God is in me
as the sun is in the color
and fragrance of a flower —
the light in my darkness,
the Voice in my Silence.

•

HELEN KELLER, 1880–1968
American writer and scholar

The reason why birds can fly and we can't

is simply that they have perfect faith,

for to have faith is to have wings.

•

JAMES M. BARRIE, 1860–1937
Scottish dramatist and writer

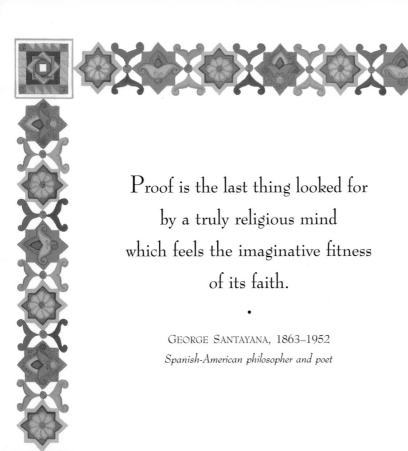

Proof is the last thing looked for
by a truly religious mind
which feels the imaginative fitness
of its faith.

.

GEORGE SANTAYANA, 1863–1952
Spanish-American philosopher and poet

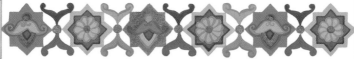

*F*aith in ourselves and faith in God —
that is the secret of greatness,
for God is Love.

•

SAI BABA
Indian spiritual master

Yes, I have doubted. I have wandered off the path. I have been lost. But I have always returned. It is beyond the logic I seek. It is intuitive — an intrinsic, built-in sense of direction. I seem to find my way home. My faith has wavered but has saved me.

•

HELEN HAYES, 1900–1993

American actress

*God has made many doors
opening into truth which
He opens to all who knock upon them
with the hands of faith.*

•

KAHLIL GIBRAN, 1883–1931
Lebanese poet, artist and mystic

Faith is the bird

that feels the light

when the dawn is dark.

•

RABINDRANATH TAGORE, 1861–1941
Indian poet and philosopher

If you have abandoned one faith,
do not abandon all faith.
There is always an alternative
to the faith we lose.
Or could it be the same thing
under another mask?

•

GRAHAM GREENE, 1904–1991
English novelist

The suffering and agonising moments through which I have passed over the last few years have also drawn me closer to God. More than ever before I am convinced of the reality of a personal God.

•

MARTIN LUTHER KING, 1929–1968
American civil rights leader and Baptist minister

Ask, and it shall be given to you;

seek and ye shall find;

knock and it shall be opened to you.

•

MATTHEW 7:7

A
PHILOSOPHY
OF LIFE

Be a good human being, a warm-hearted affectionate person. That is my fundamental belief. Having a sense of caring, a feeling of compassion will bring happiness or peace of mind to oneself and automatically create a positive atmosphere.

•

DALAI LAMA, b. 1935
Tibetan spiritual leader

It makes all the difference in the world to your life whether you arrive at a philosophy and a religion or not. It makes the difference between living in a world which is merely a constantly changing mass of phenomena and living in a significant, ordered universe.

•

MARY ELLEN CHASE, 1887–1973
American educator and author

I believe in one God and no more,
and I hope for happiness beyond this life.
I believe in the equality of man;
and I believe that religious duties
consist in doing justice, loving mercy
and in endeavouring to make
our fellow creatures happy.

•

THOMAS PAINE, 1737–1809
English-born American political writer

I expect to pass through this life but once. If, therefore, there be any kindness I can show or any good thing I can do to any fellow being, let me do it now and not defer or neglect it, as I shall not pass this way again.

•

WILLIAM PENN, 1644–1718
English Quaker and founder of Pennsylvania, USA

When I do good, I feel good.
When I do bad, I feel bad.
That's my religion.

•

ABRAHAM LINCOLN, 1809–1865
President of the United States of America

At the end of your life, you will never regret not having passed one more test, not winning one more verdict or not closing one more deal. You will regret time not spent with a husband, a friend, a child or parent.

·

BARBARA BUSH, b. 1925
First Lady of the United States of America

So many gods, so many creeds,

So many paths that wind and wind

While just the art of being kind

Is all the sad world needs.

•

ELLA WHEELER WILCOX, 1850–1919

American writer and poet

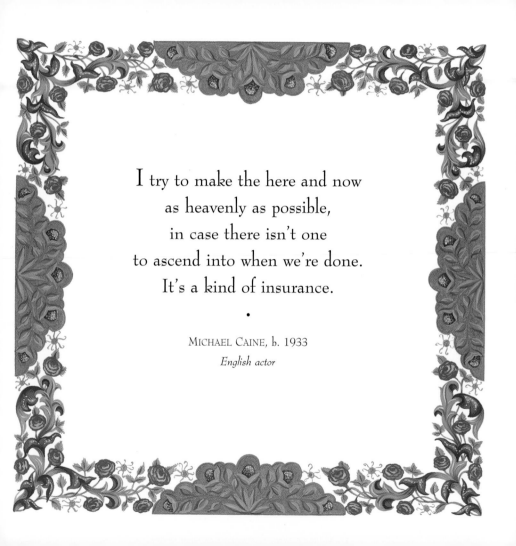

I try to make the here and now
as heavenly as possible,
in case there isn't one
to ascend into when we're done.
It's a kind of insurance.

•

MICHAEL CAINE, b. 1933
English actor

The ideals that have lighted my way and, time after time, have given me new courage to face life cheerfully have been Kindness, Beauty and Truth.

•

ALBERT EINSTEIN, 1879–1955
German-born American physicist

Do all the good you can,

By all the means you can,

In all the ways you can,

In all the places you can,

At all the times you can,

To all the people you can,

As long as ever you can.

•

JOHN WESLEY, 1703–1791
English evangelist and founder of Methodism

For my part,
I believe in the forgiveness of sins
and the redemption of ignorance.

•

ADLAI STEVENSON, 1900–1965
American lawyer, statesman and UN representative

LETTING
IT GO

Hate is like acid.
It can damage the vessel
in which it is stored
as well as destroy the object
on which it is poured.

•

ANN LANDERS, b. 1918
American advice columnist

The reason to forgive is for our own sake. For our own health. Because beyond that point needed for healing, if we hold onto our anger we stop growing and our souls begin to shrivel.

•

M. SCOTT PECK, b. 1936
American psychiatrist and writer

Here is a rule to remember in the future,

when anything tempts you to be bitter:

not, 'This is a misfortune' but

'To bear this worthily is good fortune'.

•

MARCUS AURELIUS, 121–180 AD

Roman emperor and philosopher

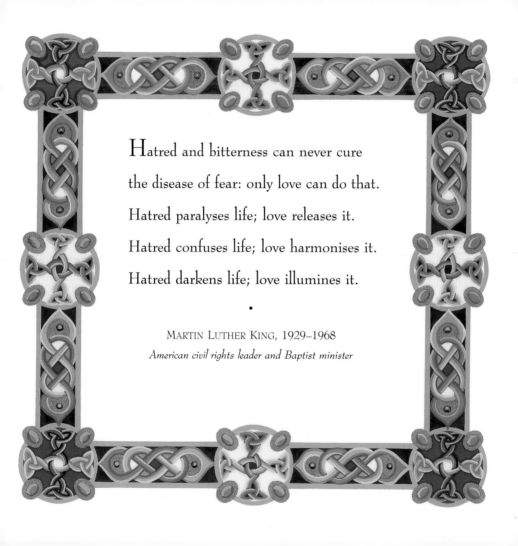

Hatred and bitterness can never cure

the disease of fear: only love can do that.

Hatred paralyses life; love releases it.

Hatred confuses life; love harmonises it.

Hatred darkens life; love illumines it.

•

MARTIN LUTHER KING, 1929–1968
American civil rights leader and Baptist minister

Man should forget his anger
before he lies down to sleep.

•

THOMAS DE QUINCEY, 1785–1859
English writer

Treat anger like a good meal. Take your time and digest it slowly. Listen to good music for hours after, and then drift off to a good night's sleep. In the light of a new day look at your anger again.

Then think carefully before you act...or you could end up with severe indigestion.

•

SARA HENDERSON, b. 1936
Australian outback station manager and writer

Forgiveness is the key

to action and freedom.

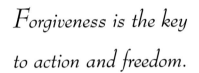

•

HANNAH ARENDT, 1906–1975
German-born American political philosopher

Hatred rarely does any harm to its object.
It is the hater who suffers.
His soul is warped and his life poisoned
by dwelling on past injuries or
projecting schemes of revenge.
Rancour in the bosom
is the foe of personal happiness.

•

LORD BEAVERBROOK, 1879–1964
Canadian-born British newspaper owner

You have no idea of the tremendous release and deep peace that comes from meeting yourself and your brothers totally without judgement.

·

A Course in Miracles

He that cannot forgive others

breaks the bridge over which

he must pass himself;

for every man has need

to be forgiven.

·

THOMAS FULLER, 1608–1661
English clergyman and writer

The man who opts for revenge should dig two graves.

•

CHINESE PROVERB

LOVE

Love gives naught but itself
and takes naught but from itself.
Love possesses not
nor would it be possessed;
for love is sufficient
unto love.

•

KHALIL GIBRAN, 1833–1931
Lebanese poet, artist and mystic

I define love thus: the will to extend oneself for the purpose of nurturing one's own or another's spiritual growth.

•

M. SCOTT PECK, b. 1936
American psychiatrist and writer

The heart benevolent and kind

most resembles God.

·

ROBERT BURNS, 1759–1796
Scottish poet

Spread love everywhere you go;
first of all in your own home.
Give love to your children,
to your wife or husband,
to a next door neighbor...
Let no one ever come to you
without leaving better and happier.

•

MOTHER TERESA OF CALCUTTA, 1910–1997
Albanian-born missionary

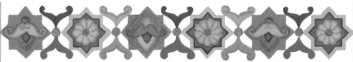

Let brotherly love continue.
Be not forgetful to entertain strangers,
for thereby some have entertained
angels unawares.

.

HEBREWS 13:2

The rule for all is perfectly simple. Do not waste time bothering whether you 'love' your neighbor; act as if you did. As soon as we do this we find one of the great secrets. When you are behaving as if you loved someone you will presently come to love him.

•

C. S. LEWIS, 1898–1963

Irish-born English academic, writer and critic

Above all,

love each other deeply,

because love covers

a multitude of sins.

•

PETER 4:8

WORDS OF
WISDOM

He that would live

in peace and ease

must not speak all he knows

nor judge all he sees.

•

Benjamin Franklin, 1706–1790
American statesman and author

All that we are is the result of what we have thought; it is founded on our thoughts, it is made up of our thoughts. If a man speaks or acts with a pure thought, happiness follows him like a shadow that never leaves him.

•

BUDDHA, 563–483 BC
Indian religious leader and founder of Buddhism

When you arise in the morning
Give thanks for the morning light.
Give thanks for your life and strength.
Give thanks for your food,
And give thanks for the joy of living.
And if perchance you see no reason for
giving thanks,
Rest assured the fault is in yourself.

·

NATIVE AMERICAN SAYING

*Show love to all creatures
and thou wilt be happy;
for when thou lovest all things,
thou lovest the Lord,
for He is all in all.*

•

HINDU SPIRITUAL TRADITIONAL

No man can live happily
who regards himself alone,
who turns everything to his own
advantage. Thou must live for another,
if thou wishest to live for thyself.

•

SENECA, c. 4 BC–65 AD
Roman philosopher, dramatist, poet and statesman

I t's only when we truly know and understand that we have a limited time on earth — and that we have no way of knowing when our time is up — that we will begin to live each day to its fullest, as if it was the only one we had.

•

ELISABETH KÜBLER-ROSS, b. 1926
Swiss-born American psychiatrist